Paper Wasp

Monica Harris

Heinemann Library
Chicago, Illinois

Designed by Ginkgo Creative, Inc.
Printed and bound in the United States by Lake Book Manufacturing, Inc.
Photo research by Scott Braut

07 06 05 04 03
10 9 8 7 6 5 4 3 2 1

Library of Congress Cataloging-in-Publication Data
Harris, Monica, 1964-
  Paper wasp / Monica Harris.
     p. cm. — (Bug books)
Summary: Describes the physical characteristics, habits, life cycle, and natural environment of the wasp that utilizes special paper-making cells in constructing its nest.
Includes bibliographical references (p.   ).
  ISBN: 1-40340-767-3 (HC), 1-40340-991-9 (Pbk.)
  1. Paper wasps—Juvenile literature. [1. Paper wasps. 2. Wasps.] I. Title. II. Series.
  QL568.V5 H27 2003
  595.79'8—dc21
                            2002004026

Acknowledgments
The author and publishers are grateful to the following for permission to reproduce copyright material:
p. 4 Mark Cassino; p. 5 Scott Camazine/Oxford Scientific Films; pp. 6, 7, 12 Stephen McDaniel; p. 8 James P. Rowan; p. 9 B. Borrell/FLPA; pp. 10, 19, 27 James H. Robinson; p. 11, 24 William E. Ferguson; p. 13 Kaweath Oaks Preserve; p. 14 Alan Weaving/Ardea London; p. 15 Silvestris Fotoservice/FLPA; pp. 16, 21 Bill Beatty/Painet Inc.; p. 17 Adam Hart-Davis/Science Photo Library; p. 18 John Chard/Stone/Getty Images; p. 20 K. G. Vock/OKAPIA/Oxford Scienfific Films; pp. 22, 23 Scott Braut; p. 25 Dr. P. Marazzi/Science Photo Library; p. 26 Mike Price/SAL/Oxford Scientific Films; p. 28 Steve Hoffmann; p. 29 Raphael Carter.

Illustration, p. 30, by Will Hobbs.
Cover photograph by Mark Cassino.

Every effort has been made to contact copyright holders of any material reproduced in this book. Any omissions will be rectified in subsequent printings if notice is given to the publisher.

Special thanks to Dr. William Shear, Department of Biology, Hampden-Sydney College, for his review of this book.

Some words are shown in bold, **like this**. You can find out what they mean by looking in the glossary.

Contents

What Are Paper Wasps?

Paper wasps are **insects**. They chew wood to make a **paste.** They use this paste to build small boxes, called **cells**. Each cell has six sides. The cells are their homes.

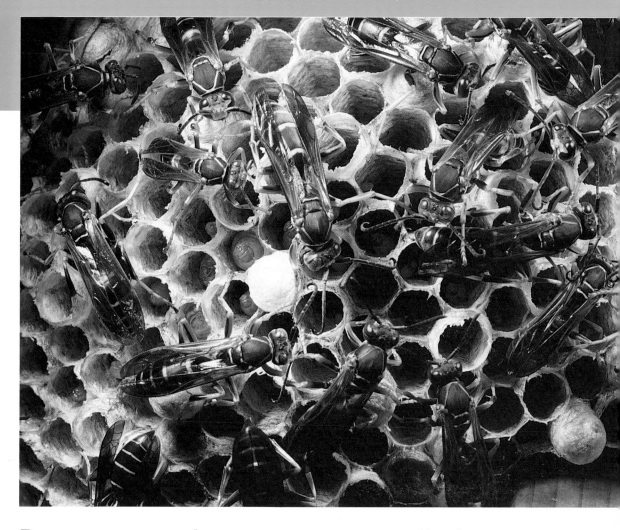

Paper wasps live in a group called a **colony.** Each colony has a **female queen.** The other females are called **workers. Male** wasps are called **drones.**

What Do Paper Wasps Look Like?

The paper wasp body has a head, a **thorax,** and an **abdomen.** The head has two eyes and two **antennae.** The thorax has six legs and four wings.

Paper wasps can be brown, black, or dark red. Most have yellow spots or stripes. Their wings are brown or black. Their bodies are very thin.

How Big Are Paper Wasps?

Two paper wasps lined up are as long as your little finger. They can spread their wings to look bigger.

Female wasps have **stingers.** Stingers are sharp and give off **poison.** Wasps use them to guard the nest. **Drones** do not have stingers.

How Are Paper Wasps Born?

Paper wasps **hatch** from eggs. Only **queen** wasps can lay eggs. In the spring, the queen builds a small nest. She lays one egg in each paper **cell.**

Wasp eggs are small, white, and shaped like a chicken egg. The queen does not cover the top of the cell. In about two weeks, **larvae** hatch from the eggs.

How Do Paper Wasps Grow?

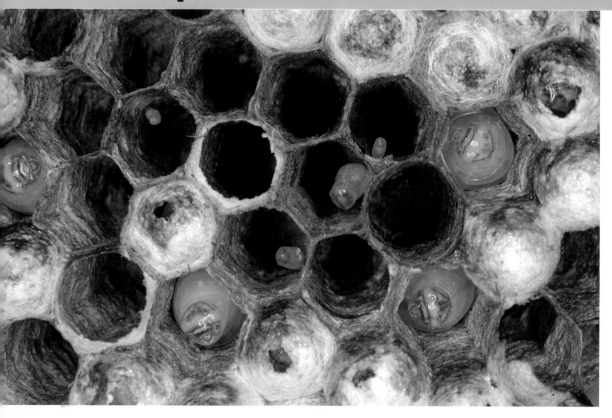

Larvae look like fat worms. After eighteen to twenty days, they make **silk** and cover the tops of their **cells.** Now they are called **pupae.**

The first pupae to **hatch** become **workers.** They build more cells and feed the larvae. Later, the other pupae will hatch into new **queens** and **drones.**

What Do Paper Wasps Eat?

Wasp **larvae** cannot leave the nest to eat. The **queen** and **workers** feed them. They chew **insects** and spit them up for the larvae. **Pupae** do not eat.

Adult paper wasps eat caterpillars, flies, and butterfly larvae. They drink juice from flowers and fruit. Wasps like sweet foods.

Which Animals Attack Paper Wasps?

Spiders, birds, beetles, and other wasps eat paper wasps. Raccoons and ants are also **predators.** If the **queen** is killed, a new queen takes over.

Many people think wasps will hurt them. They spray the wasps with **insecticide.** Insecticide is a **poison.** If you don't want wasps close to you, have someone remove the nest.

Where Do Paper Wasps Live?

Paper wasps live in warm places. They make nests in trees, attics, or on the sides of buildings. They build their nests where they are safe from wind, rain, and people.

A nest looks like an umbrella with a handle on the top. The opening of each **cell** faces the ground. A small paper thread holds the nest up.

How Do Paper Wasps Move?

Paper wasps have claws at the ends of their legs. The claws help them hold on to the nest. They also help the wasp walk on a wet piece of fruit.

Wasps use their four wings to fly.
They fly to find good food and wood.
The wings look thin, but they are
very strong.

How Long Do Paper Wasps Live?

Queen wasps live for about twelve months. Before winter, they **mate** with the **drones.** Then they find a safe place to stay for the winter. It is safe under the tree bark.

Workers and drones live for about two months. They die when it gets cold. The empty nest will not be used again.

What Do Paper Wasps Do?

Wasps may scare you, but they are good for gardens. They eat **insects** like caterpillars and moths. These insects can kill plants.

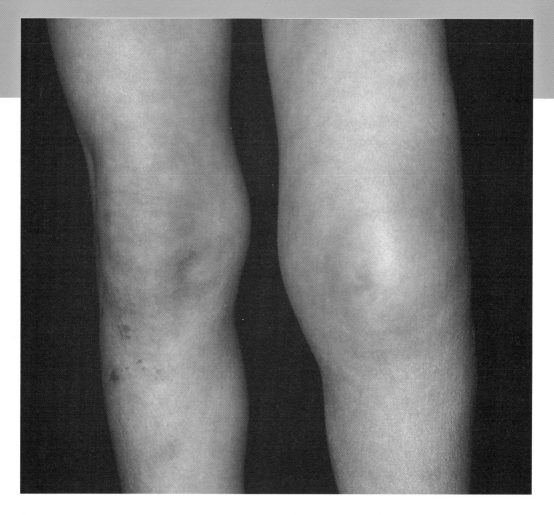

Female wasps use their **stingers** to **protect** the nest from **predators.** Wasps can sting over and over again. A sting makes the skin **swell.**

How Are Paper Wasps Special?

Wasps are small, but they have strong jaws to chew wood. They mix the wood with **saliva.** This makes the **paste** for their nests.

Each wasp has a job. The **queen** starts the nest and lays her eggs. **Workers** make the nest bigger and feed the **larvae. Drones mate** with the queens.

Thinking about Paper Wasps

Wasps are fun **insects** to watch, but they don't like to be bothered. If you find a paper wasp nest, why should you leave it alone?

This wasp is in a garden. Are wasps good for gardens? Or are they bad for gardens? Why?

Paper Wasp Map

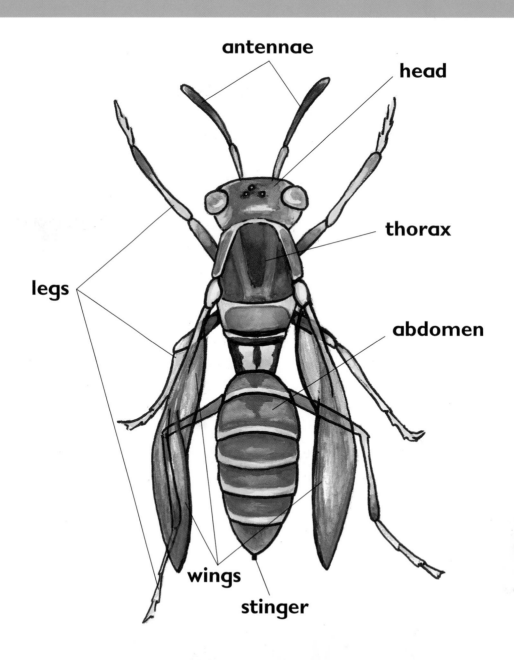

antennae

head

thorax

abdomen

legs

wings

stinger

Glossary

abdomen belly of an animal

adult grown-up

antennae thin tubes on an insect's head that can be used to smell and touch

cell small paper box that is part of a nest

colony group of wasps

drone male wasp

female girl

hatch to come out of an egg

insect animal with six legs and three body parts

insecticide chemical that kills insects

larvae (one is a **larva**) first part of an insect's life, when it looks like a worm

male boy

mate when a male and a female come together to make babies

paste gooey, gluelike substance

poison something that can hurt you or make you sick

predator animal that hunts other animals for food

protect keep safe

pupae (one is a **pupa**) part of an insect's life when it turns into an adult

queen female wasp that can lay eggs

saliva watery liquid that comes from the mouth

silk thin, shiny thread

stinger sharp body part

swell get bigger

thorax chest of an insect's body

worker female wasp that does not lay eggs

More Books to Read

Totally Amazing Wasp Book. Westminster, Md.:
    Golden Books, 2001.

Hartley, Karen and Chris Macro. *Bee.* Des Plaines, Ill.:
    Heinemann Library, 1998.

Index